CIRCLE / SQUARE

T.J. McLemore

CIRCLE / SQUARE
An Autumn House Book

All rights reserved.
Copyright © 2020 by T.J. McLemore
Typeset in Minion Pro
Cover design by Kinsley Stocum
Cover art sources:
Photo by Roger Fenton, The Valley of the Shadow of Death. *1855*
Illustration from The First Six Books of the Elements of Euclid *by Oliver*
Byrne, "In a Given Circle to Inscribe a Square." 1847
Printed in the USA
No part of this book can be reproduced in any form whatsoever
without written permission from the publisher, except in the case
of brief quotations embodied in critical reviews or essays.
For information about permission to reprint, contact Autumn House Press,
5530 Penn Avenue, Pittsburgh, PA 15206.

ISBN: 978-1-938769-66-5

All Autumn House books are printed on acid-free paper and meet the
international standards of permanent books intended for purchase by libraries.

Autumn House Press receives state arts funding
support through a grant from the Pennsylvania
Council on the Arts, a state agency funded by the
Commonwealth of Pennsylvania, and the
National Endowment for the Arts, a federal agency.

www.autumnhouse.org

CIRCLE / SQUARE

T.J. McLemore

AUTUMN
HOUSE PRESS
PITTSBURGH, PA

for K

Table of Contents

I wanted to see how our image fuses
Into the circle and finds its place in it.

—Dante

In this language there are no words for how the real world
collapses.

—Joy Harjo

Surfaces

i. apophenia

When the Bradford pear trees lift
their silver skirts, it's a sure sign
of rain, and seeing the little hairs

in the small of your back
again is like clouds over the sea.
Sometimes I can believe this world

wants to be known. Today
buds swell from deadwood,
leaves spin like pinwheels

at the lips of a skinny kid.
Every surface reflects us, but
the face I see in the mirror

is not the face I show you.
Light breaks on blown water,
sparring with shadow, capricious

spring carries the limestone
smell of the Guadalupe River over
the maples of Jamaica Pond,

and I'm gone, lost in the contours
of days like leaves in a book.
What's left to interpret? The path

of rising smoke, the way
a face folds in time, the scrawl
your hand makes down the margin—

ii. fata morgana

Here at the land's edge, remember?
It pulled back its sheets for us,

riffled the pages on its broken spine.
Layers sheer as mica, rough as the surf

the ocean surges in and sighs through.
Distance hands its judgments down

in blue. Brown hair blown across a face is sweet,
sure, but this photo almost missed you. Blur

of eyes, empty mouth, you stretch into
a trick of the light, the sea wind lifting

each strand of you to the folded hills,
the landscape gathering what it can.

M-Theory;
or, A Piece for Eleven Strings

(where M stands for magic, mystery, or membrane, according to taste)
—EDWARD WITTEN

the body too, impossibly tuned and tensioned—

all of us crimped, folded and thrumming just so, they say,

like a trillion trillion guitars or glass harmonicas, tiny

symphonies of sound—so why not metaphysics? and maybe

it was a lonely voice that started it all, a single word

that set everything to spinning out in ripples, these circles

we know so well: as all water ends up in the sea, for a time,

as planets will spiral into stars, be turned to light

(so what is death but a change of state?)—set free

in time, no rhythm or body, pushing back the void, still

humming whatever this song is we all run on, and run to

Ghost Particle

How light gives us shape and tears at us.
This Polaroid ruined, streaked by stray rays and snow.
Or perfected: your one eye a coal, the other a star.
The horse's fence a brushstroke of white, a blaze. Scarring his face.
The exposure doubles: two horses, four, beside you.
Your hands everywhere on the animal, your face unresolved.

Too many poses to reconcile.
Too many angles to consider from a single point in space.
Snow blindness is like that, a buildup of glare from all sides.
And the packed ice under us, which keeps nothing.
Or like the smallest particles that stream from the sun.
They run us through and through, touching no part of us.

Golden Section

I'd like to get away from earth awhile

—ROBERT FROST

(a body)

like all matter has a way of spiraling

down once you build it up, one line

at a time. Sheila must have thought so.
She knew how to cut an angle,

symmetry giving onto proportion,
and we all took note. Such an attentive
teacher, how she held my hand

to help me chord a circle, lightly
touching my shoulder, bending
straight at the waist in a perfect
bisection. Halfway through the year,
she disappeared. Her geometry

class taught me to wish that John,
from his prison on Patmos, had imagined
another heaven: eternity packed in
the florets of a daisy, sectioned in a curve
of nautilus, a long arc of walrus tusk.
Surely he'd traced the veins in a leaf, seen
golden sculptures of the old gods—
like his cell, John's heaven was a cube.

Word got around after she'd posted bail
and returned to school: Sheila climbed
the Eiffel Tower. Blitzed one night, she lit
a line of 151 across Lamar, our town's
main drag—sectioned it straight across,
no doubt humming the jingle she'd taught us:
a plus b is to a, just as a is to b.
She fled on foot to the civic center's
sixty-foot tower. In class she'd showed us
the real Eiffel's perfect proportions, how
in our replica they got the ratios wrong.
Still up she climbed, up until she was foiled
by the big red cowboy hat on top

and the police pulled her back to earth.

Meditation on Form and Uncertainty

The "path" comes into being only because we observe it.
—WERNER HEISENBERG

No, your wits can't fix this.
      The closer you look
the more you're wrong.
        John measured the walls
of heaven, but down here
      a line can always divide,
pulling you in, and in: as soon
      as you know one side
of the story, everything
      changes. You thought matter
was a pitcher to hold
      a good wine, but it's sprung
a leak—the more you pour in,
      the faster it drains.
Even the words you say
      back away from you,
gone. A faith once cast off
      can't be called back.

There's nothing for it,
      all these circles to square—

four points to the compass,
        just one turn
to the wheel, a course
        and its representations
to live by, a weak beam
        to see by the light of.
Steered by symbol
        and rumor, moved by lines
traced along the hands
        and brow, the counting
of stalks, imperfections
        in the skull. The maps
you hang to tack your pins to
        and search for your own
face in, the distances
        you fear might hold
all there is of you.

Zeno

The crux of the matter was infinity
tucked into every shoreline, every map

we wanted to make. I always hoped
the world might unclose its round heart

for me if only I could meet it halfway.
Sure, maybe every arrival is an illusion,

like touch, small negatives always holding us
a little apart. But I couldn't possibly live

and believe it. Not tonight, anyway,
my feet crunching on the crushed granite

of the museum walk, the glass-walled
building dark. A fox slides into the bushes

at the edge of the courtyard. The crepe myrtles
bloom, silent on their many stems. Streetlights scrawl

wild sine waves on the reflecting pool
that rise and fall with me as I walk, doubling

on the smooth surface of the water pouring
over the pool's lip to the black basin below.

It's that old oscilloscope on the present,
a reminder that this is the one world,

that this is our time in it. Tonight
I can almost believe our lives touch and return

to the world like the water falling to rejoin
this pool, each negative canceled out

by the miraculous sweep of a line above an axis.
If you can't see the circles close to hold you,

unbeliever, the dark water yawns,
you're just not standing far enough away.

Love Poem: Suspension

Heat seeps out at angles, making mirages
over the neighbors' roofs. Shifting axes
promise fall. Like summer, the shed

behind our house slides to an imprecise
end, held tight by vines of ivy that trellis
its sides and drag their feet, stretching

south, leaning into this slow sure wreck,
pull of soil, the earth that longs for us all…

From beyond the yard cicadas ratchet up
the dark over porch and shed and summer
itself. In the last light we look up to the lines

of live wires sagging overhead, tying
us together, what power we imagine
never far, ungraspable above us—

Accretion / Aftermath

The things that move us most all break
under their own weight, imploding
on themselves like the jellyfish
you saw as a kid that washed up too high
on shore, gone liquescent. Or the year
we watched summer stretch out each night

from our porch, dazed out of bleached
lawns and heat lightning, parching
and tanning us into August only to fall
apart and freeze over. Dissonance
in music, walls of wrecked melody

that tangle, shatter, and resolve at last
like the release of a long-held breath.
Even the heart pulls apart
in its hunger to possess itself,

a figure I guess for what draws me
to the aftermath. To dissolution.
The galaxy's brightest stars

don't burn out but collapse
so completely they devour

themselves, leaving light as detritus

to orbit the hole they left behind.

Entanglement Sonnet

It is, after everything, our need to remember.
I held your camera, you steadied my hand.
We found the tree with the lights in it.
The grandstand by the river.
A speedboat with fishermen.
Cottonwoods let go their long exhalations.
Children approached, then ran away giggling.

We linger in the wood duck's lighting,
the twitch and burst of a redwing in reeds,
late sun climbing like power lines up the bluff,
the cattail heads heavy as with swarms of bees,
and thumbing these photos, I know you know
that even lone atoms, once paired, will cry
to each other across a void, and change.

Thermodynamic Meditation

A humid winter, rain on rain. From the house
Zeppelin I revolves on blown speakers,
ice blending too fast with the whiskey
in whorls like heat haze, Dad's heavy
spool-top table rocking on new legs.

The plank-ends of this sodden porch
begin to curl, pulling out their nails.
I'll swap in new boards next summer,
as every atom in me will change.

I ebb into this small town: a narrow
cracking patch of lawn, the rotten
shed following the rain down
like Plant's voice follows Page,

like I followed you here.
A redbird on the buckled
fence even sings along,
wind, wings and light, this

old alchemy in the trees.
Nothing I can create
or destroy. Word

and world. Each
in decaying

orbit.

Self-Portrait as Posthuman

What matters most is where you're standing. Across the party
or on the other side of the bar, things measure differently.
No changing the rules:
where there's an equal sign, to get one thing you have to give up another.
Light flees. It runs from you.
If you could move fast enough, this party would go on and on,
and still you'd chase it, always faster, as
all things blur to white in a mess of moment.

Meditation on the Mandelbrot Set

We rediscover and repeat

creation's one original phrase.

An atom's nucleus looks like

the compound eye of a fly looks

like a bin of beach balls looks like

a mammatus cloud

looks like a star cluster,

which probably figures

the multiverse, a knot of cells

splitting, each and every one,

at a blink of the smallest eye.

*

Cut away to Paris, Texas,

third-grade weekend,

an afternoon walk.

Down behind the cattail lake

at the spillway where beavers

built and rebuilt their dam,

I nearly fell into an old cistern

behind the cabin

hidden under a patch of bluestem—

a crack of rotten wood, the ground went,

and Dad caught my arm.

I wonder now: if I'd fallen,

what scene would I have landed in—

slid down what new sky

over the same red grasses swaying

a lake ringed by tall cattails

gone to seed, beavers burrowing

through their secret dam

and Dad's face suddenly

above me, his hand

reaching into the mouth

of a forgotten well

to pull me up

Parallax

It's high time to clean the kitchen,
the stovetop snaked with fat

caramel rivers, the charred smell
revived with water—sweet on savory

ginger and lemon, salt and brown sugar
sauce E made from scratch that we spooned

over peaches. She's on a flight to Boston.
I scrape the black crust, wanting

to follow her back, stuck instead
cleaning up sweetness that ran

over. Everything that pricks me
to feel sure feels a lot like homesickness.

The heart unstill: the stars you've learned
to string together shift when you step

off the plane, every story you believe in
untrue from any other angle. Sure, I grew up

in this little Baptist town. Studied up north
and came back with new sight. I scrub

the skillet, scour it with steel wool
and put it over a flame to dry, then pull it off

to oil the surface. I reach to lift the stove's iron
grate—twining my fingers in—and hear the hiss

of burning skin. I drop the hot metal.
It brands streaks on the linoleum floor.

So then: do you track your focus to the heart
or the hand? By the time the kitchen's clean,

the thick air outside has cooled. I stretch
for a run on the neighborhood's brick streets,

my fingers a patchwork of Band-Aids.
Azaleas in every flowerbed boast their reds

and whites and pinks as teenage girls
in period dresses wave to passersby

from their porches. They do not wave
to me. As I peel off my soaked shirt

rounding the block home, I squash
an earthworm in the street that tried

to make it across the hot bricks
but burned up in the middle distance.

Lighted

Shadows thatch the porch and pattern
the siding. The house's paint is peeling,

curling into and out of shadow, dropping

to the cracking concrete below. Mid-afternoon,
mid-season. The lawn leaches color,

shunting what life's left to roots underground.

Some days I can't blink through
the glare, can't shake off the strength

entropy draws from the leavings of each breath.

Some days I study old photos of myself,
watch the dark circles creep under my eyes.

Some evenings I sit on this porch until

the air cools, the shadows resolve
to one persistent gray present tense

and wait for the fireflies to start their slow

dance above the yard. For my heart
to hang there in that glow for a moment.

Love Poem: Pareidolia

Pathetic, you say, how I always
anthropomorphize the rain. Thin legs

running down the windows,
tiny knuckles knocking, wanting

to find a way inside. Not a trace
of self-consciousness in this

condensation and fall, and I envy it,
the simple ambition to let go

and flow through every crack and pore.
Maybe gravity's the figure for all desire,

each hoped-for rush of release
or prayer for a little death, our solitary

need to watch our lives flash by us
as we fall. But I'm never alone with you

in this waterlogged city, watched
from café chairs and on the T, walking

on campus, in the Fens. Today the world
subverts my need to name it, my simple

understanding of x because it happens like y.
The dull lapping of the bay is only

and unmistakably itself, muted by distance.
The hills shed the rain and bear up

the old brownstones, every line
of the city diffused in this thick drizzle.

The public garden grays and shrinks
away. Light looks swallowed

by the landscape. All colors bleed.
Sure, the world holds its secrets close,

but look: over the horizon-line of roofs,
the sun begins to burn through

the fog. Light breaks over Beacon Hill,
and for a moment each atom of the city's

skin becomes a tiny star, the rain
transfigured into a billion mirrors,

currents of light pulsing white down the scars
in the street, arcing over the old cemetery

and out to sea. The kids next door
burst onto the balcony where I sit

on this thrift-store reading chair, run down
the stairs through the brilliant sheets of rain,

squealing. I pull on a cigarette and stare,
fixed by these changes, the longed-for face

that watching always draws from some sky.

Reduced

The same math that mounds
this thunderhead pins us down,

peels back the stubborn veil
of the flesh—but only what's shrouded

in dark can be blinded
by light. Inside every body

a hundred miles of miracle.
Heat lightning leaps the world's

synapses out beyond the mountains.
A single bolt arcs up from

the cedar's crown down the street
to meet a flash shattering

its alien script across the sky.
Quick blackout of the senses,

concentric blink, cold shock
to wipe the insides blank.

The forecast says rain for days.
Sometimes the world is profligate,

holding nothing back, renewing
the passing wonder we are.

Notes

"Surfaces." The second section ("fata morgana") borrows a line from T. S. Eliot's "Ash Wednesday."

"M-Theory; or, A Piece for Eleven Strings." M-Theory attempts to reconcile the five versions of Superstring Theory, which seek to unify the fundamental forces of nature by proposing that all matter is made up of tiny loops of string that vibrate in eleven dimensions (which are then folded and compacted into the four we experience).

"Golden Section" is formally based on the Fibonacci Sequence (0, 1, 1, 2, 3, 5, 8, 13), derived from the golden ratio first defined by Euclid as the ratio between two numbers whose sum has the same relationship to one of the quantities as the two original quantities have to each other ($[a + b] / a = a / b$). The poem riffs on Robert Frost's "Birches."

"Meditation on Form and Uncertainty" draws on divinatory methods and the Uncertainty Principle, which states that the momentum and position of quantum objects cannot simultaneously be known. Our inability to know both values is not due to technological or methodological limitations; it seems to be a fundamental quality of the universe that it resists our attempts to know it.

"Meditation on the Mandelbrot Set" takes its form and conceit from the Mandelbrot Set, a set of numbers that, when mapped, results in a recursive fractal. As a fractal visualization, the set can be zoomed infinitely; any detail in the set will allow an endless "journey" further down into the image, and the forms encountered will recur with slight variations at each successive level of zoom. The poem also engages with the multiverse interpretation of quantum mechanics, which proposes that our universe splits at each moment, resulting in a sea of universes in which every possible permutation of reality exists.

Acknowledgments

My gratitude to the editors of the following journals who first shepherded the poems in this chapbook into the world, some in slightly different forms:

32 Poems: "Reduced"
The Carolina Quarterly: "Love Poem: Suspension"
COUNTERCLOCK Journal: "Surfaces [fata morgana]"
The Greensboro Review: "Entanglement Sonnet"
JuxtaProse: "Meditation on the Mandelbrot Set"
Lake Effect: "Accretion / Aftermath," "Love Poem: Pareidolia"
Michigan Quarterly Review: "M-Theory; or, A Piece for Eleven Strings"
Nimrod: "Lighted"
Prairie Schooner: "Golden Section"
RHINO Poetry: "Zeno"
Salamander: "Meditation on Form and Uncertainty"
Tinderbox Poetry Journal: "Thermodynamic Meditation"
Tupelo Quarterly: "Ghost Particle"
Willow Springs: "Parallax"
The Worcester Review: "Surfaces [apophenia]"

"M-Theory; or, A Piece for Eleven Strings" was reprinted as a feature on *Poetry Daily* on September 16, 2017.

I want to extend special thanks to everyone who generously gave themselves and their time to shape these poems, providing much-needed encouragement and criticism over the years: Karen McClellan, my partner and first reader; my parents and my sister; Lisa Hiton, Dan Kraines, and Calvin Olsen, my dear friends, companions, and readers, my constant champions; Matthew Allen, who first showed me the path; Sarah Harrison, who believed; Mark Jarman, for his invaluable comments on early drafts of several of these poems; Robert Pinsky and Louise Glück, who provided the workshop constraints in which several of these poems found their fledgling forms; and to Autumn House Press for their work on this volume, particularly Mike Good for his insightful edits, and to Kinsley Stocum for the gorgeous cover art.

About the Author

T. J. McLemore's poems appear in *New England Review, Crazyhorse, The Adroit Journal, 32 Poems, Prairie Schooner, Michigan Quarterly Review,* and other journals, and have been featured on *Poetry Daily,* selected for *Best New Poets,* and nominated for the Pushcart Prizes. He has received awards and fellowships from the Sewanee Writers' Conference, Poetry by the Sea, Boston University, and *Crab Orchard Review.* McLemore is a doctoral student in English and Environmental Humanities at the University of Colorado Boulder.

New & Forthcoming Releases

under the aegis of a winged mind by makalani bandele ♦ Winner of the 2019 Autumn House Poetry Prize, selected by Cornelius Eady

Circle / Square by T. J. McLemore ♦ Winner of the 2019 Autumn House Chapbook Prize, selected by Gerry LaFemina

Hallelujah Station and Other Stories by M. Randal O'Wain

Grimoire by Cherene Sherrard

Further News of Defeat: Stories by Michael X. Wang ♦ Winner of the 2019 Autumn House Fiction Prize, selected by Aimee Bender

Skull Cathedral: A Vestigial Anatomy by Melissa Wiley ♦ Winner of the 2019 Autumn House Nonfiction Prize, selected by Paul Lisicky

No One Leaves the World Unhurt by John Foy ♦ Winner of the 2020 Donald Justice Prize, selected by J. Allyn Rosser

In the Antarctic Circle by Dennis James Sweeney ♦ Winner of the 2020 Autumn House Rising Writer Prize, selected by Yona Harvey

Creep Love by Michael Walsh

The Dream Women Called by Lori Wilson

To view our full catalog, please visit <u>autumnhouse.org</u>